I0697814

PRACTICAL GUIDE TO WEALTH MASTERY

UNLEASH YOUR FINANCIAL POTENTIAL AND TRANSFORM YOUR LIFE

Break Free from Financial Struggles with Confidence and Ease Using a Proven 6-Week Plan

NICK A, PETERSON

Copyright © 2024 Nick, A Peterson

All rights reserved. No part of this publication may be reproduced, distributed, or transmitted in any form or by any means, including photocopying, recording, or other electronic or mechanical methods, without the prior written permission of the publisher, except in the case of brief quotations embodied in critical reviews and certain other noncommercial uses permitted by copyright law.

INTRODUCTION

EMBRACING A WEALTH MINDSET

Welcome to " PRACTICAL GUIDE TO WEALTH MASTERY," where the transformation begins with a simple yet profound shift in mindset. In this introduction, we lay the foundation for your journey towards financial abundance by exploring the power of embracing a wealth mindset.

In a world often characterized by scarcity and limitation, cultivating a wealth mindset is not merely about accumulating riches; it's about adopting a mindset of abundance, possibility, and empowerment. It's about recognizing that true wealth encompasses far more than just financial resources—it encompasses health, relationships, personal growth, and contribution to the world.

Throughout this book, we'll delve into the principles and practices that will enable you to break free from scarcity thinking and embrace abundance in all areas of your life. From shifting your beliefs about money to reframing your relationship with success and failure, each chapter will guide you towards a deeper understanding of what it means to truly thrive.

As we embark on this journey together, I invite you to approach each page with an open mind and a willingness to challenge old paradigms. By embracing a wealth mindset, you'll not only unlock new opportunities for financial success but also cultivate a sense of fulfillment, purpose, and joy that extends far beyond your bank account.

Are you ready to step into your power and claim the abundant life you deserve? Let's begin.

CHAPTER ONE

RECOGNIZING LIMITING BELIEFS

WEEK 1: UNDERSTANDING YOUR RELATIONSHIP WITH MONEY

Money, a mere medium of exchange, yet it holds immense power over our lives. How we perceive money, our beliefs about it, and the stories we tell ourselves about our ability to manage it shape our financial reality. In this first week of our journey towards wealth mastery, we delve deep into the subconscious beliefs that may be holding us back from financial abundance.

SECTION 1: THE POWER OF BELIEF

Beliefs are like invisible scripts that dictate our thoughts, actions, and ultimately, our outcomes. Many of these beliefs are formed during childhood, influenced by our family, society, and cultural norms. Some beliefs serve us well, empowering us to pursue our goals with confidence.

However, others can be limiting, trapping us in patterns of scarcity and fear.

SUBSECTION 1:1: UNCOVERING YOUR MONEY STORY

In this subsection, we guide readers through a process of introspection to uncover their money story. By reflecting on past experiences, family dynamics, and societal influences, readers gain insight into the beliefs that have shaped their relationship with money. This exercise lays the foundation for identifying and challenging limiting beliefs.

SUBSECTION 1:2: COMMON MONEY MYTHS AND MISCONCEPTIONS

Here, we explore prevalent money myths and misconceptions that may be hindering financial progress. From the belief that money is inherently evil to the notion that wealth is reserved for the lucky few, we debunk these myths with evidence-based research and practical examples. By exposing the fallacies behind these beliefs, readers are empowered to adopt a more empowering mindset.

SECTION 2: IDENTIFYING LIMITING BELIEFS

With a deeper understanding of the power of belief, we shift our focus to identifying and challenging specific limiting beliefs that may be sabotaging financial success.

SUBSECTION 2:1: MONEY AND SELF-WORTH

One common limiting belief revolves around the idea that our self-worth is tied to our net worth. In this subsection, we explore the detrimental effects of equating financial success with personal value and provide strategies for separating self-esteem from monetary wealth. By fostering a sense of intrinsic worthiness, readers can free themselves from the pressure to constantly chase external validation through material possessions.

SUBSECTION 2:2: FEAR OF SCARCITY VS. EMBRACE OF ABUNDANCE

Another prevalent belief is the fear of scarcity—the belief that there will never be enough to go around. Here, we delve into the psychological roots of scarcity mindset and its impact on financial decision-making.

Through exercises and practical techniques, readers learn to shift from scarcity to abundance mindset, recognizing the vast opportunities available for wealth creation and abundance.

SECTION 3: CHALLENGING AND REWRITING BELIEFS

Having identified limiting beliefs, it's time to challenge them head-on and rewrite the script for financial success.

SUBSECTION 3:1: COGNITIVE RESTRUCTURING TECHNIQUES

Drawing from cognitive-behavioral therapy and positive psychology principles, we introduce readers to cognitive restructuring techniques. Through mindfulness, reframing, and affirmations, readers learn to identify negative thought patterns and replace them with empowering beliefs that align with their financial goals.

SUBSECTION 3:2: **CULTIVATING A GROWTH MINDSET**

Central to challenging limiting beliefs is cultivating a growth mindset—the belief that intelligence, abilities, and success are not fixed traits but can be developed through effort and perseverance. Through real-life examples and inspiring stories, readers gain insight into the power of resilience, grit, and continuous learning in achieving financial mastery.

As readers conclude the first week of their journey, they are equipped with the tools and insights to recognize and challenge limiting beliefs that may be hindering their financial progress. Armed with a newfound sense of empowerment and possibility, they are ready to embark on the next phase of their wealth mastery journey with clarity, confidence, and determination.

CHAPTER TWO

SETTING FINANCIAL GOALS THAT ALIGN WITH YOUR VALUES

WEEK 2: CULTIVATING A MINDSET OF ABUNDANCE

In Week 1, we explored the beliefs that shape our relationship with money. Now, as we enter Week 2 of our journey towards wealth mastery, we shift our focus to the practical aspect of setting financial goals. By aligning our goals with our values, we lay the groundwork for a fulfilling and purpose-driven financial journey.

SECTION 1: THE POWER OF VALUES-BASED GOAL SETTING

At the core of setting meaningful financial goals lies the alignment with our values—the principles and ideals that guide our decisions and actions. In this section, we delve into the importance of values-based goal setting and its role in fostering a sense of purpose and fulfillment in our financial endeavors.

SUBSECTION 1:1: IDENTIFYING YOUR CORE VALUES

The journey begins with self-discovery. Through introspection and reflection exercises, readers uncover their core values—the fundamental principles that define who they are and what they stand for. By gaining clarity on their values, readers can make informed decisions about their financial goals, ensuring that they align with their deepest desires and aspirations.

SUBSECTION 1:2: CONNECTING VALUES TO FINANCIAL GOALS

With a clear understanding of their values, readers learn how to translate them into tangible financial goals. Whether it's achieving financial independence, supporting a cause they believe in, or creating a legacy for future generations, each goal is infused with meaning and purpose. By anchoring their goals in their values, readers cultivate a sense of motivation and commitment that propels them forward in their financial journey.

SECTION 2: THE SMART APPROACH TO GOAL SETTING

While values provide the foundation, practicality is essential in goal setting. In this section, we introduce readers to the SMART criteria—a framework for setting goals that are Specific, Measurable, Achievable, Relevant, and Time-bound. By applying this framework, readers ensure that their goals are not only meaningful but also actionable and attainable.

SUBSECTION 2:1: SPECIFICITY IN GOAL SETTING

We guide readers through the process of refining their goals to make them specific and clearly defined. By breaking down broad aspirations into concrete objectives, readers gain clarity on what they want to achieve and how they plan to get there. Specific goals serve as a roadmap, guiding readers towards success with precision and focus.

SUBSECTION 2:2: MEASURING PROGRESS AND SUCCESS

In this subsection, readers learn the importance of measuring progress towards their goals. By establishing benchmarks and tracking their financial journey, readers gain valuable insights into their progress and areas for improvement. Regular monitoring allows for course correction and adjustment, ensuring that readers stay on track towards their desired outcomes.

SUBSECTION 2:3: ENSURING ACHIEVABILITY AND RELEVANCE

Achieving financial goals requires a balance between ambition and feasibility. Here, we help readers assess the achievability and relevance of their goals, taking into account factors such as resources, time constraints, and personal priorities. By setting goals that are both challenging and realistic, readers set themselves up for success while maintaining alignment with their values and aspirations.

SUBSECTION 2:4: **SETTING TIMELY DEADLINES**

Finally, we emphasize the importance of setting deadlines for achieving financial goals. By establishing clear timelines and milestones, readers create a sense of urgency and accountability that motivates action. Timely deadlines prevent procrastination and encourage consistent progress towards desired outcomes.

As readers conclude Week 2 of their wealth mastery journey, they emerge with a clear understanding of the power of values-based goal setting and the practical tools needed to translate their aspirations into reality. With their goals firmly in place, aligned with their values and guided by the SMART criteria, readers are ready to embark on the next phase of their financial journey with confidence, clarity, and determination.

CHAPTER THREE

CREATING A BUDGET THAT WORKS FOR YOU

WEEK 3: MASTERING MONEY MANAGEMENT

As we progress in our journey towards financial mastery, we come to Week 3—a pivotal stage where we dive into the fundamental aspect of money management: creating a budget. A well-crafted budget serves as the cornerstone of financial success, providing a roadmap for managing income, expenses, and savings effectively. In this chapter, we explore the principles and strategies for creating a budget that aligns with your financial goals and lifestyle.

SECTION 1: UNDERSTANDING THE IMPORTANCE OF BUDGETING

Budgeting is not merely about restricting spending; it's about gaining control over your finances, maximizing your resources, and achieving your financial aspirations. In this section, we delve into the significance of budgeting and its role in fostering financial stability, reducing stress, and building wealth over time.

SUBSECTION 1:1: THE BENEFITS OF BUDGETING

We highlight the numerous benefits of budgeting, from providing clarity and transparency in financial matters to facilitating better decision-making and goal achievement. By understanding the advantages of budgeting, readers are motivated to embrace this essential practice as a tool for financial empowerment.

SUBSECTION 1:2: THE PSYCHOLOGICAL IMPACT OF BUDGETING

Budgeting goes beyond numbers; it influences our mindset and behavior towards money. Here, we explore the psychological impact of budgeting, including its role in promoting mindfulness, discipline, and accountability. By cultivating positive money habits through budgeting, readers develop a healthy relationship with money that supports their long-term financial well-being.

SECTION 2: BUILDING YOUR BUDGET BLUEPRINT

With the foundation laid, we move on to the practical aspects of budgeting—creating a personalized budget blueprint that reflects your financial goals, priorities, and lifestyle.

SUBSECTION 2:1: ASSESSING INCOME AND EXPENSES

The first step in creating a budget is to assess your current financial situation. Readers learn how to calculate their total income from various sources and track their expenses over a specified period. By gaining clarity on their cash inflows and outflows, readers can identify areas for optimization and prioritize spending according to their values and goals.

SUBSECTION 2:2: CATEGORIZING EXPENSES

Here, we guide readers through the process of categorizing their expenses into essential and discretionary categories. By distinguishing between needs and wants, readers gain insight into their spending patterns and identify areas where they can potentially cut back or reallocate funds towards their priorities.

SUBSECTION 2:3: SETTING BUDGETING GOALS

Building on the foundation of income and expenses, readers learn how to set specific budgeting goals that align with their financial objectives. Whether it's saving for a down payment on a home, paying off debt, or building an emergency fund, readers are guided through the process of establishing actionable goals that drive their budgeting efforts.

SECTION 3: IMPLEMENTING AND MONITORING YOUR BUDGET

Creating a budget is just the first step; implementing and monitoring it is crucial for long-term success. In this section, we provide practical tips and techniques for implementing your budget effectively and tracking your progress over time.

SUBSECTION 3:1: CHOOSING A BUDGETING METHOD

We explore various budgeting methods, from traditional envelope systems to digital budgeting apps, and help readers choose the approach that best suits their preferences and lifestyle. By leveraging technology and automation, readers can streamline the budgeting process and make it more manageable and convenient.

SUBSECTION 3:2: REVIEWING AND ADJUSTING YOUR BUDGET

Budgeting is an ongoing and flexible process that necessitates frequent evaluation and modification. Here, readers learn how to conduct periodic budget reviews to evaluate their financial progress, identify areas of overspending or underspending, and make necessary adjustments to their budgeting plan. By staying flexible and responsive to changing circumstances, readers ensure that their budget remains relevant and effective in guiding their financial decisions.

As readers conclude Week 3 of their wealth mastery journey, they emerge with a comprehensive understanding of budgeting as a fundamental tool for financial success. Armed with a personalized budget blueprint and practical strategies for implementation and monitoring, readers are empowered to take control of their finances, make informed decisions, and progress towards their financial goals with confidence and clarity.

CHAPTER FOUR

INVESTING FOR LONG-TERM GROWTH

WEEK 4: ELIMINATING DEBT AND BUILDING A SOLID FOUNDATION

Entering Week 4 marks a significant shift in our journey towards financial mastery. We pivot our focus from budgeting and expense management to the proactive pursuit of wealth accumulation through investing for long-term growth. In this chapter, we delve into the principles, strategies, and best practices for building a diversified investment portfolio that aligns with your financial goals and risk tolerance.

SECTION 1: UNDERSTANDING THE IMPORTANCE OF INVESTING

Investing is the key to wealth creation and financial independence. In this section, we explore the importance of investing for long-term growth, including the role of compound interest, inflation, and market fluctuations in shaping investment outcomes. By understanding the power of investing, readers are motivated to take proactive steps towards building wealth through strategic investment decisions.

SUBSECTION 1:1: THE POWER OF COMPOUND INTEREST

Compound interest is often referred to as the eighth wonder of the world, and for good reason. We explain how compound interest works and its exponential growth potential over time. By harnessing the power of compounding, readers can amplify their investment returns and accelerate their journey towards financial freedom.

SUBSECTION 1:2: THE IMPACT OF INFLATION AND MARKET RISKS

We explore the impact of inflation and market risks on investment returns and purchasing power. Readers gain insights into strategies for mitigating these risks, such as diversification, asset allocation, and dollar-cost averaging. By understanding the dynamics of inflation and market volatility, readers can make informed decisions to preserve and grow their wealth effectively.

SECTION 2: **BUILDING A DIVERSIFIED INVESTMENT PORTFOLIO**

With a solid understanding of the importance of investing, we move on to the practical aspects of building a diversified investment portfolio that aligns with your financial goals, risk tolerance, and time horizon.

SUBSECTION 2:1: **SETTING INVESTMENT OBJECTIVES**

The first step in building an investment portfolio is to define clear investment objectives. We guide readers through the process of setting specific, measurable, achievable, relevant, and time-bound (SMART) investment goals. By aligning investment objectives with their financial aspirations, readers can create a roadmap for achieving their long-term wealth accumulation goals.

SUBSECTION 2:2: **UNDERSTANDING ASSET CLASSES**

We introduce readers to various asset classes, including stocks, bonds, real estate, and alternative investments. Readers learn about the characteristics, risk-return profiles, and diversification benefits of each asset class.

By understanding the role of different asset classes in a diversified portfolio, readers can construct a well-balanced investment strategy that optimizes risk-adjusted returns.

SUBSECTION 2:3: **IMPLEMENTING ASSET ALLOCATION STRATEGIES**

Asset allocation is the process of spreading investment capital across different asset classes to optimize risk and return. We explore various asset allocation strategies, including strategic asset allocation, tactical asset allocation, and dynamic asset allocation. Readers learn how to tailor asset allocation strategies to their risk tolerance, investment objectives, and market conditions to achieve optimal portfolio diversification and risk management.

SECTION 3: SELECTING SUITABLE INVESTMENT VEHICLES

With asset allocation in place, we move on to the selection of suitable investment vehicles to implement the investment strategy effectively.

SUBSECTION 3:1: EQUITY INVESTMENTS

We delve into the world of equity investments, including individual stocks, mutual funds, and exchange-traded funds (ETFs). Readers learn how to evaluate and select equity investments based on factors such as company fundamentals, valuation metrics, and investment objectives. By diversifying across a broad range of equity investments, readers can capture the growth potential of the stock market while mitigating individual stock risk.

SUBSECTION 3:2: **FIXED-INCOME INVESTMENTS**

We explore fixed-income investments, including government bonds, corporate bonds, and municipal bonds. Readers learn about the characteristics, credit quality, and interest rate sensitivity of fixed-income securities. By incorporating fixed-income investments into their portfolio, readers can generate stable income streams and reduce overall portfolio volatility.

SUBSECTION 3:3: **REAL ESTATE AND ALTERNATIVE INVESTMENTS**

We introduce readers to alternative investments, such as real estate, commodities, and private equity. Readers learn about the potential benefits and risks of alternative investments and how to incorporate them into their portfolio to enhance diversification and potentially boost returns. By exploring alternative investment opportunities, readers can access unique sources of alpha and further diversify their investment portfolio.

As readers conclude Week 4 of their wealth mastery journey, they emerge with a comprehensive understanding of investing for long-term growth and the practical tools needed to build a diversified investment portfolio. Armed with clear investment objectives, asset allocation strategies, and selection criteria for investment vehicles, readers are empowered to take control of their financial future, optimize their investment returns, and progress towards their long-term wealth accumulation goals with confidence and conviction.

CHAPTER FIVE

EXPLORING OPPORTUNITIES FOR PASSIVE INCOME

WEEK 5: GENERATING PASSIVE INCOME STREAMS

Entering Week 5 marks a significant milestone in our journey towards financial mastery. We shift our focus from traditional income sources to exploring opportunities for passive income—the holy grail of financial freedom. In this chapter, we delve into the principles, strategies, and best practices for generating passive income streams that can supplement or replace earned income, allowing you to build wealth and achieve financial independence over time.

SECTION 1: UNDERSTANDING PASSIVE INCOME

Passive income is income generated with minimal effort or active involvement on your part. In this section, we explore the concept of passive income and its role in creating financial freedom and flexibility. By understanding the different types of passive income and their potential benefits, readers gain insight into the power of passive income as a wealth-building tool.

SUBSECTION 1:1: TYPES OF PASSIVE INCOME

We introduce readers to various types of passive income, including rental income, dividends, interest income, royalties, and affiliate marketing. Readers learn about the characteristics, advantages, and challenges of each passive income stream and how to leverage them to achieve their financial goals.

By diversifying across multiple passive income streams, readers can create resilient income sources that provide stability and growth over time.

SUBSECTION 1:2: THE PASSIVE INCOME MINDSET

Generating passive income requires a shift in mindset from trading time for money to creating systems and assets that generate income passively. We explore the mindset shifts and habits necessary for building passive income streams, including patience, persistence, and a willingness to invest time and resources upfront for long-term rewards. By adopting a passive income mindset, readers can overcome limiting beliefs and embrace the potential for financial abundance and freedom.

SECTION 2: BUILDING PASSIVE INCOME STREAMS

With a solid understanding of passive income, we move on to the practical aspects of building passive income streams that align with your skills, interests, and resources.

SUBSECTION 2:1: REAL ESTATE INVESTING

Real estate investing is one of the most popular and proven ways to generate passive income. We explore various real estate investment strategies, including rental properties, real estate investment trusts (REITs), and crowdfunding platforms. Readers learn how to evaluate real estate investment opportunities, analyze rental income potential, and manage rental properties effectively to generate passive income and build wealth over time.

SUBSECTION 2:2: DIVIDEND INVESTING

Dividend investing involves investing in dividend-paying stocks and funds to generate passive income through regular dividend payments. We guide readers through the process of selecting dividend-paying stocks, assessing dividend yield and growth potential, and building a diversified dividend portfolio. By focusing on high-quality dividend stocks with a track record of consistent dividend payments, readers can create a reliable income stream that grows over time through dividend reinvestment.

SUBSECTION 2:3: **CREATING DIGITAL ASSETS**

In the digital age, creating digital assets is another lucrative way to generate passive income. We explore various digital asset creation opportunities, including e-books, online courses, digital products, and membership sites. Readers learn how to identify profitable niches, create valuable digital content, and market their digital assets effectively to generate passive income and scale their online business over time.

SECTION 3: **MAXIMIZING PASSIVE INCOME POTENTIAL**

With passive income streams in place, we move on to strategies for maximizing their income potential and optimizing returns.

SUBSECTION 3:1: SCALING PASSIVE INCOME STREAMS

We explore strategies for scaling passive income streams, including reinvesting profits, expanding into new markets, and leveraging automation and outsourcing. By scaling passive income streams, readers can increase their income potential and accelerate their journey towards financial independence.

SUBSECTION 3:2: PASSIVE INCOME TAX STRATEGIES

We delve into passive income tax strategies, including tax-efficient investing, retirement account contributions, and tax deductions for passive income activities. Readers learn how to minimize their tax liability on passive income and maximize their after-tax returns to achieve their financial goals more efficiently.

We provide practical tips and techniques for managing passive income portfolios, including portfolio rebalancing, diversification, and risk management. By actively managing passive income portfolios, readers can optimize their returns, mitigate risks, and adapt to changing market conditions to achieve long-term financial success.

As readers conclude Week 5 of their wealth mastery journey, they emerge with a comprehensive understanding of passive income and the practical tools needed to build and scale passive income streams. Armed with diverse passive income opportunities, a passive income mindset, and strategies for maximizing passive income potential, readers are empowered to take control of their financial future, create multiple streams of passive income, and achieve lasting wealth and financial freedom with confidence and conviction.

CHAPTER SIX

UNLOCKING YOUR EARNING POTENTIAL

WEEK 6: MAXIMIZING YOUR EARNING POTENTIAL

As we enter Week 6 of our journey towards financial mastery, we shift our focus to maximizing our earning potential—the foundation of wealth creation and financial independence. In this chapter, we delve into the strategies, techniques, and mindset shifts necessary to unlock your earning potential, increase your income, and achieve your financial goals with confidence and purpose.

SECTION 1: EMBRACING A GROWTH MINDSET

At the core of maximizing your earning potential lies the belief in your ability to grow, learn, and adapt. In this section, we explore the concept of a growth mindset and its role in overcoming limiting beliefs, embracing challenges, and pursuing continuous improvement. By cultivating a growth mindset, readers can unlock their full potential and pursue new opportunities for personal and professional growth.

SUBSECTION 1:1: THE POWER OF BELIEF IN YOUR POTENTIAL

We delve into the psychology of belief and its impact on performance, motivation, and success. Readers learn how self-limiting beliefs can hold them back from reaching their full potential and how adopting a belief in their ability to learn and grow can empower them to overcome obstacles and achieve their goals. By shifting their mindset from fixed to growth-oriented, readers can unlock new possibilities for personal and professional development.

SUBSECTION 1:2: **EMBRACING CHALLENGES AND FEEDBACK**

We explore the importance of embracing challenges and seeking feedback as opportunities for growth and learning. Readers learn how to cultivate resilience, grit, and a willingness to step outside their comfort zone to pursue new opportunities and expand their skill set. By embracing challenges and feedback with an open mind and a willingness to learn, readers can accelerate their personal and professional growth and unlock new opportunities for success.

SECTION 2: STRATEGIES FOR MAXIMIZING YOUR EARNING POTENTIAL

With a growth mindset in place, we move on to practical strategies for maximizing your earning potential and increasing your income.

SUBSECTION 2:1: INVESTING IN YOURSELF

Self-investment is the most beneficial investment one can undertake. We explore various ways to invest in yourself, including education, skills development, and personal development. Readers learn how to identify areas for improvement, set learning goals, and invest time and resources in acquiring new skills and knowledge that will enhance their earning potential and advance their career.

SUBSECTION 2:2: NEGOTIATING YOUR WORTH

In order to maximize your earning potential and obtain equitable compensation for your skills and expertise, it is vital that you negotiate your value. We provide practical tips and techniques for negotiating salary raises, promotions, and freelance rates effectively.

Readers learn how to prepare for negotiations, articulate their value proposition, and advocate for their worth with confidence and professionalism.

SUBSECTION 2:3: EXPLORING SIDE HUSTLE OPPORTUNITIES

Side hustles are an excellent way to supplement your income, pursue your passions, and diversify your income streams. We explore various side hustle opportunities, including freelancing, consulting, e-commerce, and gig economy platforms. Readers learn how to identify side hustle opportunities that align with their skills, interests, and resources and how to successfully launch and grow a side hustle while balancing their other commitments.

SECTION 3: BUILDING WEALTH-BUILDING HABITS

Maximizing your earning potential requires discipline, consistency, and the cultivation of wealth-building habits. In this section, we explore habits that can help you increase your income, manage your finances effectively, and achieve your financial goals.

SUBSECTION 3:1: TIME MANAGEMENT AND PRODUCTIVITY

Time management and productivity are essential for maximizing your earning potential and making the most of your time and resources. We provide practical tips and techniques for managing your time effectively, setting priorities, and staying focused and motivated. Readers learn how to eliminate time-wasting activities, set clear goals, and develop routines and systems that optimize their productivity and efficiency.

SUBSECTION 3:2: FINANCIAL PLANNING AND GOAL SETTING

Financial planning and goal setting are critical for maximizing your earning potential and achieving your financial goals. We explore the importance of setting clear financial goals, creating a budget, and developing a plan for achieving your goals. Readers learn how to prioritize their financial goals, track their progress, and make informed decisions that align with their long-term objectives.

SUBSECTION 3:3: CONTINUOUS LEARNING AND GROWTH

Continuous learning and growth are essential for maximizing your earning potential and staying competitive in today's rapidly evolving economy. We explore the importance of lifelong learning, professional development, and staying up-to-date with industry trends and innovations. Readers learn how to invest in their personal and professional growth, seek out new opportunities for learning and development, and stay ahead of the curve in their field.

As readers conclude Week 6 of their wealth mastery journey, they emerge with a comprehensive understanding of the strategies, techniques, and mindset shifts necessary to maximize their earning potential and achieve their financial goals. Armed with a growth mindset, practical strategies for increasing their income, and wealth-building habits, readers are empowered to unlock new opportunities for personal and professional growth, increase their income, and achieve financial independence with confidence and purpose.

CONCLUSION

As we reach the conclusion of **"Practical Guide to Wealth Mastery: Unleash Your Financial Potential and Transform Your Life,"** it's essential to reflect on the journey we've embarked upon together. Throughout these pages, we've explored the principles, strategies, and mindset shifts necessary to achieve financial mastery and unlock the path to a life of abundance, prosperity, and fulfillment.

In our quest for wealth mastery, we've delved deep into the core components of financial success, from understanding our relationship with money to setting clear financial goals, mastering money management, and investing for long-term growth. We've explored the power of passive income and the strategies for maximizing our earning potential, empowering us to create multiple streams of income and build wealth over time.

But beyond the practical strategies and techniques lies a deeper truth: wealth mastery is not just about accumulating riches—it's about living a life of purpose, fulfillment, and contribution. It's about aligning our financial goals with our values, passions, and aspirations, and creating a legacy that extends far beyond our bank accounts.

As you close this book, I encourage you to carry forward the lessons learned and apply them to your daily life. Embrace a mindset of abundance and possibility, cultivate discipline and resilience, and take inspired action towards your financial goals with unwavering determination.

Keep in mind that achieving expertise in money is a continuous process, rather than a final goal. It necessitates the qualities of patience, perseverance, and a dedication to ongoing development and acquisition of knowledge. Along the way, you may encounter challenges and setbacks, but with the right mindset and strategies, you have the power to overcome any obstacle and achieve your dreams.

I invite you to continue your journey with courage and conviction, knowing that you have the knowledge, skills, and resources to create the life of abundance and freedom you desire. May this book serve as a guiding light on your path to wealth mastery, empowering you to unleash your financial potential and transform your life for the better.

Here's to your success, prosperity, and fulfillment in all aspects of life.

www.ingramcontent.com/pod-product-compliance
Lightning Source LLC
Chambersburg PA
CBHW070221260726
48658CB00006BA/2131